WIL[...]
DIALECT

A selection of words and anecdotes
from around Wiltshire

by
Linda Fernley

BRADWELL
BOOKS

Published by Bradwell Books
9 Orgreave Close Sheffield S13 9NP
Email: books@bradwellbooks.co.uk

British Library Cataloguing in Publication Data:
a catalogue record for this book is available from
the British Library.

1st Edition

ISBN: 9781909914605

Print: Gomer Press, Llandysul, Ceredigion SA44 4JL

Design and artwork by: Andrew Caffrey

Photograph Credits: Past & Present Publications,
Linda Fernley and where indicated iStock

'Here is the heart of our island … the fibres of England unite in Wiltshire, and did we condescend to worship her, here we should erect our national shrine.'

E. M. Forster

Introduction

Wiltshire is a county in the south-west of England, bordered by Hampshire, Dorset, Berkshire, Somerset, Gloucestershire and Oxfordshire. It is landlocked, boasts almost 1,400 square miles (3,500 sq km), and is characterised by its high downland and beautiful wide valleys. Salisbury Plain is famous as the location of the ancient landmarks of Stonehenge – where druids still gather each year at summer and winter solstices – and the stone circles at Avebury, among others, and is also renowned as the training ground for the British Army.

The view of **Salisbury Cathedral** across the water meadows of the River Avon has been voted the loveliest view in England, and was famously painted by renowned artist, JOHN CONSTABLE, from the gardens of the Bishop's Palace.

Much of this rural county is given over to agriculture, although industry has become increasingly important; **Swindon** – the major manufacturing town – is one of the fastest-growing urban areas of England. There are a large amount of 'timeless' rural villages with thatched, limestone-built cottages, and a vast selection of cosy country pubs offering open fires in winter and traditional English food and drink.

Constable's Salisbury Cathedral Creative Commons

Wiltshire was once a part of 'Wessex', the West Saxon kingdom. West Saxon became one of the most influential dialects that make up Old English; however, there are, or certainly were, several distinctions in the Wiltshire form, and the dialect is characterised by its very noticeable 'r' sounds.

As the population has become more mobile over the past 75 years, sadly, along with many other local dialects around the UK, the use of a Wiltshire dialect has steadily decreased.

However, there are still many words that were common in Old or even Middle English that can still be found in use today. For instance, *'thee'* is often used instead of *'you'* and is sometimes abbreviated to *'ee'*, as in *'I is off fer a drink – is 'ee comin?'* You will often hear *'I'* instead of *'me'*, and will find that *'I am'* is sometimes replaced with *'I be'*, and often an erroneous *'s'* is placed at the end of a word: '*I sees that'*. And *'s'* is often pronounced as *'z'*, as in *'zommet is wrong with this'*, while *'v'* can be heard instead of *'f'*, as in *'What be a-lollupin' about like that vor?'* A letter *'t'* is often pronounced as a *'d'*, as in *'I be tellin ee, dat dractor needs new tyres'* ('I'm telling you, that tractor needs new tyres')!

The following glossary is a selection of words taken from what older local Wiltshire people either remember or still use, and from words first recorded in *Glossary of Words Used in the County of Wiltshire*, complied by GEORGE EDWARD DARTNELL and THE REV. EDWARD HUNGERFORD GODDARD in 1893.

After the glossary, you'll find snippets about Wiltshire life that I hope give a flavour of the rich diversity of the county, both past and present.

Linda Fernley 2015

Glossary

A

Ael – all

Anbye – at some time in the future time: *'I be main busy now, but I'll do't anbye.'*

Anighst – near: *'Nobody's bin anighst us since you come.'*

Anneal (nealded) – heated oven

Arkin – listening

Art'noon – afternoon

Athout – without, outside

Away with – endure: *'Her's that weak her can't away with the childern at no rate!'*

Ax – ask

Ayeet – eight

B

Ballarag, bullyrag – to abuse or scold

Bams – rough gaiters of pieces of cloth wound about the legs, much used by shepherds and others exposed to cold weather

Bane – sheep-rot

Baned – afflicted with sheep-rot

Bargain – small landed property or holding, e.g. house, garden, land

Bawsy, borsy or bozzy – coarse, as applied to the fibre of cloth or wool: *'Bozzy-faced cloth bain't good enough vor I.'*

Been, bin – because, since; a corruption of 'being': *'Bin as he don't go, I won't.'*

Billy-buttons – idiot

Black-Bob – cockroach

Blind-house – a jail or lock-up

Bobbish – in good health: *'Well, an' how be 'ee to-day?'* *'Purty bobbish, thank 'ee.'*

Bog – toilet

Brown – a gloomy day

Budgy – moody, sulky

Bulragging – nagging

Baker's van, Hullavington Past & Present

C

Cack-anded – left-handed or clumsy

Caterpillar – a cockchafer (maybug)

Chaff – worthless uncomplimentary words

Cham – to chew: *'Now cham thee vittles up well.'*

Chamrag – gossip

Chatrin – talking

Chitterlings – pigs' entrails when cleaned and boiled

Chore – a narrow passage between houses

Clobber – clothes

Cloddy – thick, plump, stout

Clot – a hard lump of dry cow-dung, left on the surface of a pasture

Coney-burry – a rabbit's hole

Curly-buttons – woodlice

D

Dainty – evil-smelling: *'That there meat's ter'ble dainty.'*

Daps – plimsolls, trainers

Devil-screecher – the common swift

Dicky – (1) of vegetables, decayed; (2) of persons or plants, weakly or in ill-health

Diddikoys – Gypsies

Diddle – to cheat

Do – two

Dree – three

Dru – through

Dudman – a scarecrow

Dunner – a man or animal 'done for' and past hope:
'Thuck old sow be a dunner; her'll be dead afore night.'

Skaters on the Avon at Amesbury 1909 Past & Present

E

Eass (sometimes Yees) – an earthworm

Emmet – ant

English parrot – green woodpecker

F

Faggot, fakket – (1) A woman of bad character is 'a nasty stinking faggot (or vaggot)'. Often used in a milder sense, as in *'You young vaggot – what be slapping the baby vor?'* (2) A rissole of chopped pig's-liver and seasoning

Firk – (1) to worry mentally, to be anxious: *'Don't firk so'* or *'Don't firk yourself'*; (2) to be officiously busy or inquisitive

Fitty – in good health: *'Howbe'ee?' 'Ter'ble fitty.'*

Flustrated – (1) taken aback, flustered: *'A didn't zay anything … but a looked a leetle flustrated like'*; (2) tipsy

Fluttery – of weather, uncertain, showery: *'Tull be a main fluttery hay-making to-year, I warnd.'*

Frickle, friggle – to potter about at little jobs, as an older person might: *'I bain't up to a day's work now; I can't do nothing but frickle about in my game.'*

G

Gammock – to lark about, to play the fool, frolic

Gaulpin – looking, staring

Gawpus – a stupid person, fool

Goosegog – gooseberry

Gossipin – idle talk

Grizzle – to complain

Girt or gurt – very big, great

Grouty – of the sky, thundery, threatening rain

H

Hacker/hagger – tremble as with the cold

Hagged – haggard, worn out, exhausted-looking. *'Her've a had a lot to contend wi' to-year, and her's hagged to death wi't aal.'*

Half-baked – stupid

Hanglers – the hooks by which pots and kettles are suspended over open fireplaces in old cottages and farmhouses

Hocksy, hoxy – dirty, muddy, miry: *'It's about two miles in vine weather; but when I's hocksey like this, we allows a mile vor zlippin' back!'*

Hoop – the bullfinch

Horse-stinger, hosstenger – dragonfly

Hudgy – clumsy

Hudmedud – scarecrow

Hullocky – *Hullo! look here!* An exclamation of surprise, or calling attention to anything

Hurkle – to crowd together

I

In-a-most – almost: *'It inamwoast killed our bwoy, Sam.'*

Conservative Fete, Harnham, near Salisbury 1909 Past & Present

J

Jarl – to quarrel, to *'have words'*

Jaw-bit – food carried out to the fields by labourers, to be eaten as a morning snack

Jibbets – small bits and pieces

Jonnick – honest, fair, straightforward in dealings

Junk – a hunch of bread and cheese, or a lump of wood or coal

K

Keck – to retch as if sick, to cough

Kiver – a cooling receptacle used in brewing

Knacker – to snap the fingers

L

Latter lammas – a person who is repeatedly late

Lollop – laze about

Loppetty – weak, not feeling oneself

M

Maggotty – frisky, playful

Main – good or excellent

Malbro-handed – awkward

Marnin – good morning

Mere – a boundary line or bank of turf

Mickle – much

Mid, med – might or may

Missus – wife

Mommick – scarecrow

Mooned-up – spoilt

Moonraker – applied to a person born and bred in Wiltshire (see p23)

Moots – roots of trees left in the ground

Mop – a fair for hiring servants

Mucker – miserly person

Muddle-fuss – a persistent meddler in other people's affairs

Muggeroon – mushroom

Castle Combe Past & Present

N

Nanny-fodger – a prying or interfering person
Narration – fuss, commotion: *'Wha' a narration about n'owt'*
Naumpey – foolish, weak-minded
Newsmonger – a gossip
Ninny hammer – a stupid or silly person
Nistn't – needn't
Nor (or nur) – than, as in *'E be better nur that.'*
Nummet – lunch

O

Ogmeoid – person who thinks they're better than others
Oss – horse
Over-right, vorright – opposite to

P

Pantony – pantry
Parlous – cunning
Plock – a log of firewood perfectly shaped to fit the grate
Pot-walloper – someone possessing house with a *'pot-well'* (fireplace) for cooking. In Wootton Bassett pot-wallopers had voting rights
Pounceful – masterful, self-willed
Power – a quantity of anything as in *'a power o' volk'* – a number of people
Privet – to pry
Pucksey – quagmire, messy, muddy
Puddle or piddle about – to potter about, doing little jobs of no great importance
Purdy – pretty

Q

Quest, quist – woodpigeon

Quiddle – a fussy person

Bradford on Avon - Co-op van Past & Present

R

Rag-mag – beggar

Rawny – thin or weak

Revel – pleasure fair, parochial festival

Rhaa – hungry, ravenous

Rick – twist, as in to twist an ankle

Rinnick – the smallest and worst pig of a litter

Rough – feeling unwell

Rumpum-scrumpum – kind of musical instrument, made of a piece of board, with an old tin tied across it as a bridge, over which the strings are strained; played like a banjo or with a bow

S

Scag – to snag or tear

Scaultin – rushing or straining

Scrammy – awkward or stiff

Screech – mistle thrush

Screws – rheumatism

Scruple – to squeak or creak

Shandy – a pointless argument

Sharpish – considerable: *'I be eighty-vive to-year, an' 'tis a sharpish age.'*

Shitabed – dandelion

Showl – shovel

Shrammed – extremely cold

Simmin – it seems

Skew-wiffey – bent or crooked

Skimmenton – a serenade of rough music played to express disapproval in cases of great scandal or immorality

Skit – a passing shower

Slewed, slewy – drunk

Slox, slocks – to waste; to steal from employers

Smother – a weed and rubbish fire in a garden

Sno – you know, or just you

Snotty – a slight crisp frost

Snuff-rag – a pocket-handkerchief

Spuddle – to stir about, to fuss about at doing trifles: *'He's allus a-spuddling about like, but there yen't nothen to show for't, sez I.'*

Squiffy – slightly tipsy

Staid – of mature age, elderly

T

Taiters – potatoes

Tang – to pull a bell

Teart – (1) painfully tender, sore, as a wound; (2) stinging, as a blister

Teg – sheep

Teg-man – a shepherd: *'I'm a teg-man in the employ of Mr White.'* WILTS COUNTY MIRROR, 28 October 1892

Thee – you

Theezelf – yourself

Thine – yours

Three-pound-tenner – name given by bird-catchers around Salisbury to the cheveral variety of goldfinch, it being more valuable than the ordinary kind

Thunderbox – outside toilet

Thur – there

Tidunt – it's not

Ting-tang – a small church-bell

Toad-stabber – a badly blunted knife

Townie – not from the countryside

To-year, T'year – this year: *'I bain't a-gwain' to set no taters to-year.'*

Trammel hawk – peregrine falcon

Tranter – haulier

Trumpery – weed bed

Tuther – the other

Twinge – a long flat cake or loaf of bread

U

Unbelieving – disobedient

Unt – isn't

Harvesting, Bradenstoke area c1910 Past & Present

V

Vamplets – gaiters
Varmut – child or creature
Var – four
Varty – forty
Vather – father
Vinney – mouldy, as applied to bread or cheese
Vittle – any sort of food that is ready to eat
Vive – five

W

Weffet, wevet – a spider
Weigh-jolt – a see-saw
Wench – woman
White-house – a dairy
Wiltshire weed – the common elm
Wivelly – undecided, wavering, fickle and untrustworthy
Womble – to wobble about from weakness
Wooster-blister – a smack in the face or box on the ear
Wun – one
Wusted – looking very ill, grown worse

Y

Yardland – quarter of an acre (a quarter of an acre was a

'landyard' wide)

Yarn – tale or story

Yees – an earthworm

Yer/yertiz – here/here it is, or your

Yuckers – baby birds in nest

Z

Zammy – a simpleton

Zeven – seven

Zix – six

Zizeman – tax man (excise man)

Zummit – something

Maypole dancers, Devizes c1910 Past & Present

Poems, Rhymes, and Moonrakers!

Wiltshire's best-known poet and carriage builder, EDWARD SLOW *(1841–1925)*, was born and bred in Wilton, and would later become mayor of his beloved hometown. Throughout his life in Wilton and Salisbury, he captured in verse the everyday lives of rural people, all in the Wiltshire dialect as it was spoken.

'The Wiltshire Moonrakers' is a poem from *Wiltshire Rhymes: A Series of Poems in the Wiltshire Dialect (1881)*. It tells of a folk legend in which two villagers, intent on avoiding the heavy taxes on spirits, ride up to Bristol and smuggle back a few barrels for the local pub. When their cart topples over on a bridge, the barrels fall into a pond and, just as the two 'girt chaps' are retrieving their bounty, the excise men show up. The quick-thinking smugglers pretend they're trying to rake out a wheel of cheese, which is actually the moon's reflection on the water! Rolling their eyes at the simple country folk, the excise men leave them to their antics. The villagers, of course, have the last laugh, and to this day Wiltshire folk are proud to call themselves 'moonrakers' – so much so that the location of the pond in the story is hotly contested, with many villages claiming it as their own.

This poem really captures Wiltshire's dialect – and of course we all like to see victory going to the underdog!

The Wiltshire Moonrakers

Down Vizes way zom years agoo,
When smuggal'n wur nuthen new,
An people wurden nar bit shy,
Of who they did their sperrits buy.
In a village liv'd a publican,
Whi kept an Inn, The Pelican,
A man he wur, a man a merrit
An his neam wur Ikey Perritt.
Ael roun about tha country voke
Tha praise of thease yer landlard spoke;
Var wen any on 'em wur took bad,
They knaw'd wur sperrits could be had;
An daly it wur nice an handy,
At tha Pelican to get yer brandy.
Twer zwold as chep as tis in Vrance,
Tho a course, twer done in iggerance.

One winter, Crismis time about,
Thease lanlords tubs as ael ran out.
Zays he, this yer's a purty goo,
Var mwore what ever shall I do;
Thie smugglin Zam's a purty chap,
Ta lave I here wieout a drap;
An wen a promised dree months back,
A hooden vail ta bring me whack.
Bit praps tha zize voke voun his trail,

An med a pop'd inta jail,
Howsemdever, I'll zen and zee,
Ta marrer wats become a he.
Zoo nex day at nite he off did start,
Two girt chaps wie a donkey cart.
Ta Bristil town thay took ther way,
An got there as twer gettin day;
Tha smugglers house tha zoon voun out,
An tould'n wat they wur com about.
Ael rite, zays he, I've plenty bye,
Bit we mist keep a cuteish eye,
Var tha zize voke, they be in tha watch,
An two or dree have lately cotch.
Zoo tell woold Perritt thats tha razin
I coudden zen avore ta pleaz un.
Soo wen twur dark thase smuggler bwold,
Got dree tubs vrim a zacrit hould;
An unobsarved he purty smart,
Zoon clap'd em in tha donkey cart;
An tha top a covered up we hay,
Then zent tha chaps an cart away;
Ael droo tha streets quite zaef an zound,
Thay zoon jog'd out a Bristil town.
An vore tha vull moon ad rose,
To ther neative pleace, wur drawin close;
Wen to ther girt astonishment,
Thay met wie a awkurd accident,

In passin auver Cannins Brudge,
Tha stubborn donkey hooden budge;
Tha chaps thay leather'd well his back,
Bit a diden keer var ther attack;
Bit jibb'd an beller'd, shook his mean
Then kick'd bouth shafts right off za clane.
Up went tha cart, tha tubs vill out,
An in tha road zood roll'd about;
An vore tha chaps cood ardly look,
Ael dree ad roll'd straite in tha brook.
Well here's a purty goo zays one,
Why will, wat ever's to be done?
I'd like ta kill thic donkey quite,
If thee wurst, zays Tom, tid zar un rite.
Doost knaa wat tha matter wur?
I thinks a got a vorester;
Var I nevir knaw'd un hack like this,
Unless zummit wur much amiss.
Look at un now he's in a scare,
An gwain as hard as he can tare;
We bouth shafts danglin on tha groun,
A wunt stop till he gets wom I'm bown.
Zoo let un, I dwoant keer a snap,
Var then thay'll gace thease yer mishap;
An zen zumbiddy on tha road,
Ta help ess get wom saef tha load.
Bit zounds, while thus we do delay,

Tha tubs, begar, ull swim away;
We mist get em out at any price,
Tho' the water be as cwoold as ice.

Dwoant stan geapin zo, var goodness zeak,
Run to thic rick an vind a reak;
I thinks that I can reak em out,
Var ther thay be swimmin about.
Two reaks wur got, an then thaese two
Did reak an splaish we much ado;
Bit nar a tub diden lan,
Thay hooden zeem ta com ta han.
Zays Tom, I'm tired a tha job,
An hooden a tuck un var ten bob;
I ad a mine ta let em goo,
An zoo I will if thee hoot to.
Get out, girt stup, we mist get in,
Tho we do get wet ta tha skin.
Till never do ta let em be,
Zo tuck thee pants up roun thee knee.
Tha chaps then took tha water bwould,
Tho thay wur shram'd ni we tha could;
An jist as thay did heave one out,
Ael at once a feller loud did shout –

Hel'oh, me lads, wat up to there,
Night poachers, ah, if teant I swear.

Let goo, zays Will, I'm blow'd if tent,
Vizes excizemen on tha scent;
Push off tha tub var goodness zeak,
Get out tha brook, teak hould a reak;
Reak at tha moon a shinin zee,
An dwoant thee spake, I'll tackle he,
Bit av ad a mishap as ya see.
Comin frum Vize we donkey cart,
On tha bridge tha donk mead zudden start;
An jirk'd, an jib'd, then gied a kick,
An het bwouth shafts off purty quick.
Out went our things wich as ya zees,
Lays ael about, an yer's a cheese;
He roll'd rite on straite in thease brook,
An Tom's a reakun vor'un look!
Tha Zizeman swallered ael o't in,
An ta zee Tom reakun, gun ta grin,
Girt vool, zays he, as true's I'm barn,
Why that's tha moon, thee beest reakun vor'n
An then a busted out agean,
An zed of ael, that beat all clean;
Ta zee a crazy headed coon,
Reak at the shadder of the moon.
Will wink'd at Tom, Tom wink'd at Will,
Ta zee how nice he'd took tha pill;
Ah, zur, you med laff as long as ya please,
Bit we be zure it be a cheese.

Zee how he shows hisself za plain,
Com Tom, lets reak vor he again.
Zo slap an dash went on reakin,
While Zizeman he var vun wur sheakin;
An off a went houlden his zide,
Var longer there a cooden bide.
We grinnin his eyes did auverflow,
Ta zee thay chaps a reakin zo;
An ta think that now he'd tould em zo,
Tha girt vools hooden ther frake vergo.
Zoo up a got upon his hoss,
An as tha brudge a went across,
He zet up another harty grin,
Wen a look'd an zeed em bouth get in;
An zed girt vools till zar em rite,
If thay da ketch ther deaths ta nite.
Bit wen he ad got clane away,
Tha tubs wur got wieout delay;
And hid away, quite zeaf and zoun,
Var a dark nite wen tha moon wur down.

Then at the Pelican thease chaps,
Purty zoon wur tellen ther mishaps;
Bit ael ther troubles they vergot,
Wen they'd emptyied well tha landloards pot,
An wen he a coose did pay em well
Thease little stowry not ta tell;

Zo wen tha Zizemin nex did com,
Woold Perritt he a coose wur mum.
An in a glass did jine wie glee,
Wen Zizemin twould tha tale ta he;
Bit he laff'd mwore wen zeaf one nite
Tha tubs wur brought wom snug an tite;
An many a bumper went a round,
To think thay'd beat tha Zizemin zound.

Bit he tha tale did zoon let out
To ael the countery roun about;
An to thease day, people da teeze,
All Wilsheer voke about tha cheese.
Bit tis thay as can avourd ta grin,
To zee ow nice a wur took in.

Zoo wen out thease county you da goo,
An voke da poke ther vun at you;
An caal ee a girt Wilsheer coon,
As went a reakun var tha moon.
Jist menshin thease yer leetle stowry,
And then bust out in ael yer glowry,
That yer smeart Excisemin vresh vrum town,
Wur took in wie a Wilsheer clown.

Bicycle ride from the Swan Hotel, Bradford on Avon *Past & Present*

Carrying on the Wiltshire literary tradition today is GWEN ELLIS, who seeks to revive interest in the dialect with humorous verse that tells the stories of historical sites and local characters. Inspired by Slow, she in turn has rendered in rhyme a folk legend about how those hailing from Aldbourne came to be known as Dabchicks. It's said that, catching sight of a strange bird one day, the residents of Aldbourne called on the oldest man in the village to identify it. Having pondered the matter at length, the elder declared it to be a dabchick, now better known as the Little Grebe and a rare visitor indeed in the downlands.

As well as giving a nickname to Aldbourne residents ever since, the tale survives in *Dabchick magazine*, Aldbourne

Dabchicks Cricket Club, the Dabchick Golf Society, and Aldbourne Dabchicks Rugby Football Club.

Aldbourne Dabchicks
from ALL MY MOONSHINE (2003)

At Aldbourne, on the village pond,
A long long time ago,
A bird were seen by village folk
Just swimming to and fro.

Nobody seemed to know what 'twere,
Not even old Fred Gee,
Who said he'd seen strange birds before,
But never one like he.

Well, after much debating,
They thought of Thomas Moore,
The oldest man in Village,
He'd know what 'twere for sure.

'You'll never get him up here,'
Said Bert White, 'he's got so fat,'
'I'll get me barrow out,' said Fred,
'And wheel him up in that.'

Old Tom were very willing
When we asked him if he'd come,

He said he'd quite enjoy it,
And 'twould be a 'bit of fun'.

It were a 'bit of fun' alright,
By golly he were stout,
I'm glad old Bert gave I a hand,
Or I'd a-tipped him out.

Well finally we reached the pond,
And Tom espied the bird,
But he just sat there mesmerised,
And never said a word.

'Have you seen out like he afore?'
Said Fred, wi half a smile,
'Just wheel I round the pond,' said Tom,
'I'll tell thee in a while.'

'A Dabchick, Ah, that's what he be,'
'Come off it,' said old Fred,
'Be you quite sure that bent a name
You've made up in your head.'

Now whether he were right or wrong,
It bent for I to say,
I only know that Aldbourne folk
Be 'Dabchicks' to this day.

What's in a name?

Many Wiltshire towns take their names from Saxon settlers. They often include an element describing a place's purpose, such as *-ham* ('village') or *-bury* ('fortified place'), but a town's name might also tell us something about the natural features of the landscape or even the kind of trade that traditionally occurred there.

The Saxon settlement in **Lacock** first took root around *Bide Brook*, which flows eastwards into the Avon. The early residents gave it the name *lacuc*, meaning 'small stream'.

Lacock Abbey Author's photo

Grinder, Warminster 1906 Past & Present

Warminster refers to the River Were, added to the Saxon word for monastery, mynster, which may have existed at the present site of ST DENYS' CHURCH. The town of **Wilton** is named after the *River Wylye*, with the Saxon suffix for 'farm' or 'settlement' – the *'tun on the Wylye'*.

The origins of the oddly named **Ludgershall** are debated. The most popular meaning of the name is 'nook with a trapping spear', from the Old English *lūte-gār*, meaning a spear set up as a trap for wild animals, and the Anglian halh, a nook of land. This settlement may have had a particular association with hunting.

Trowbridge, now the county town of Wiltshire, may mean 'tree bridge', from Old English *trēow-brycg*, referring to the first bridge over the River Biss; or 'the bridge by Trowle', after a hamlet that lies to the west.

Cricklade is thought to have been named from the Celtic element craig, 'rock', and the Old English word *gelād*, 'passage', referring perhaps to the Thames river crossing found here.

Cattle Market, Cricklade 1907 Past & Present

Bradford on Avon - bridge Past & Present

Canals and waterways are significant features of Wiltshire's scenery, and it's not surprising that several towns take their names from the rivers that run through them. Bradford on Avon is a 'broad ford on the Avon', from the Saxon *brād*, 'broad' and ford, *'shallow river crossing'*.

The town of **Devizes** grew up around the castle, built in 1010 and named '*Castrum ad divisas*', or 'castle at the boundaries', by the Romans for its position on the boundaries of the manors of **Rowde, Bishops Canning** and **Potterne**.

Another town whose name stems from its castle is **Castle Combe**, from the Saxon words *castel* and *cumb*, meaning literally 'castle valley'.

A town's name can also be a clue to its agricultural history. The name **Melksham**, a place long associated with dairy farming, is thought to mean 'milk village' from the Old English *meoluc* for 'milk', while **Swindon** comes from the Old English *swīn* and *dūn*, meaning '*pig hill*', or *hill where pigs were bred*.

Several towns are believed to carry the personal names of settlers or tribal leaders, such as '*Cippa's village*' (**Chippenham**), '*Cossa's village*' (**Corsham**) and '*Pefe's island*' (**Pewsey**).

Similarly, the name **Malmesbury** probably comes from '*Maeldub's fortification*', referring to the Irish monk who is said to have founded a monastery at Malmesbury in the 7th century. A pupil of his, ALDHELM, went on to establish Malmesbury Abbey. Legend has it that the prehistoric mound at Marlborough is the burial place of KING ARTHUR's wizard MERLIN, and that the name means '*Merlin's barrow*'.

Chippenham town square Past & Present

Malmesbury Abbey Andy & Susan Caffrey

The town motto is UBI NUNC SAPIENTIS OSSA MERLINI – *'Where now are the bones of wise Merlin'*. However, it's since been suggested that the medieval term marl, 'chalky ground', may come into it, referring to the type of countryside in which the town is set.

Royal Wootton Bassett was originally known as 'Wodeton', from the Old English *wudu* for 'wood' and *tun*, a farmstead or estate. *'The farm in the wood'* was so called for being nestled within Braden Forest, which stretched as far as Malmesbury and Cricklade and still exists in part today. ALAN BASSETT –

whose signature appears on the preface of the Magna Carta – acquired the manor around 1212, and expanded the town to the extent that it now bears his name.

The name **Salisbury** means *'fortification at Sorviodunum'*, the Latin name for the Iron Age hill fort at Old Sarum, now two miles north of the town. In 1219, POPE HONORIUS III authorised a new cathedral to be built two miles away, and this 'New Sarum' became the modern Salisbury.

Wootton Bassett Past & Present

Castle Coombe by Sue & Andy Caffrey

Identity Crisis?

With the advancement of modern media, the influence of television and radio and, perhaps, a more 'educated' class, it seems that many people in Wiltshire no longer use the words that were once commonplace throughout the county. An obvious change is the way many town and village names have been spelt differently through the ages – a good example being **Urchfont**.

It's said that over the last 400 years of its recorded history the village's name has been spelt 111 different ways and probably had even more derivations before we first picked up a quill and started scribbling!

The *Urch* part of the name is said by some to originate from an old dialect word for deer, *erche*, while the font refers to a spring. Even in the 1930s, the village was **Erchfont** – and it's this spelling that can still be seen today on the plaque outside the village hall.

Some other spellings include:
in 1303 – **Archefontte**
1334 – **Icheffont**
1377 – **Lerchesfonte**
1428 – **Orchffunte**

1572 – **Vrshaunt**
1605 – **Earchfount**
and 1695 – **Ushant**

You can read the complete list by reading the village's local history pamphlet *'Urchfont – By Any Other Name'*. Here are a few other Wiltshire place names and their alternative spellings:

Burderop – Burdrop
Fisherton Anger – Fisherton Ainjer
Mildenhall – Mynoll
Sutton Veny – Venny

Wiltshire's Claims to Fame

Salisbury Cathedral houses what is widely believed to be the world's oldest working clock, made of hand-wrought iron and dating from about 1386. It has neither hands nor dials, but is designed only to strike a bell once an hour to call parishioners to service, using a system of weights and pulleys. The clock was originally housed in a separate tower, where it worked until 1884. When a new clock was installed, the old clock fell into obscurity, until it was rediscovered in 1929 and put out on display to the public. Not until 1956 was it fully restored by JOHN SMITH AND CO. OF DERBY, and is now to be found in the aisle at the Cathedral, with nearly all of its original parts, still going strong.

Magna Carta Creative Commons

The cathedral's Chapter House also holds one of the four existing 1215 copies of the **Magna Carta**, one of the most significant documents in English history. It was brought there by ELIAS OF DEREHAM, who was present at its authorisation by KING JOHN at Runnymede and entrusted with delivering ten of the thirteen copies made. The copy at Salisbury is regarded as the finest of the four surviving originals, and still bears the marks where King John's seal was placed.

The Cathedral Close is the largest in Britain and is flanked with beautiful houses, one of which used to belong to former Prime Minister, EDWARD HEATH.

The chemist and philosopher JOSEPH PRIESTLEY (1733–1804) discovered oxygen at Bowood House near Calne on 1 August 1774. He worked for the Earl of Shelburne as a librarian for the estate and as a tutor to his sons, and was given a room there which he used as a laboratory. In a series of experiments, using the sun's rays focused through a magnifying glass to heat mercury oxide, Priestley observed that a gas was produced that made a candle burn *'with an amazing strength of flame; and a bit of red hot wood crackled and burned with a prodigious rapidity'*. Though oxygen had been produced by various chemists previously, Priestley was the first to recognise it as a distinct element.

Bowood House was the seat of the Marquess of Lansdowne and its Capability Brown designed gardens boast the largest area of mown lawn in England!

Blind faith!

EILMER, a Benedictine monk of Malmesbury Abbey, attempted man's first recorded flight when he jumped from the Abbey tower in 1010 with 'wings' strapped to his arms and legs. He reportedly glided 600 feet, before spiralling back to earth and breaking his legs. Having made a full recovery, the intrepid monk was ready to try again with a few tweaks to his design, but his abbot forbade him. A kite festival and other flight-related celebrations were held in 2010 to mark 1,000 years since Eilmer embarked on his short-lived voyage!

The Flying Monk Drawn by Tim O'Brien

Say cheese!

The world's oldest surviving photograph was taken at Lacock Abbey in 1835 by WILLIAM FOX TALBOT. It is actually a photographic negative, no bigger than a postage stamp, depicting the oriel window in the South Gallery of the Abbey. Fox Talbot's work

Fox Talbot Creative commons

laid the foundations of modern photography, although he could never have foreseen that the cloisters of his old home would one day serve as the classrooms of Hogwarts in the Harry Potter films! The ambitious Talbot continued his experiments and went on to discover, in 1840, the basic positive–negative principle for recording photographs. The original negative is held at the National Media Museum in Bradford.

Nearby **Lacock village** is also famous; arriving there you could be forgiven for thinking you've just entered the scene of a recent wizard battle or turned up to meet Mr Darcy for a dance at the assembly rooms.

The village is a firm favourite with film and TV producers, most notably for its picturesque streets and historic cottages, untouched by modern alterations. The village's

Lacock village Past & Present

most famous appearances include the BBC's *Pride and Prejudice* and *Cranford*, and the films *Harry Potter and the Half-Blood Prince* and *Wolfman*.

Crop circle Creative Commons

Wiltshire is regarded as the **'world capital of crop circles'**. These are geometric rings in which the crop, usually corn, wheat, barley or rape, is systematically flattened into complex, but often beautiful patterns. The intricate designs 'miraculously' appear overnight and can be hundreds of feet in diameter. The phenomenon originates from the 1980s in North Wiltshire, and continues to capture the imaginations of many, with some claiming that they are made by extraterrestrial visitors. Even after DOUG BOWER and DAVE CHORLEY revealed, in 1991, that they were behind over 200 circles around Warminster, visitors and enthusiasts from all over the world come to the county every year to take part in crop circle tours, camps and 'night watches'.

There's even a Crop Circle Access Centre, currently housed in the Wiltshire Museum in Devizes, and new circles are documented by the Wiltshire Crop Circle Study Group, who send up planes to photograph the formations.

Bremilham Church in Malmesbury is officially the smallest 'in service' church in Britain, measuring a tiny 13 feet by 11 feet (4 x 3.5m)! A local farmer had used it to store turkeys up until the Collins family bought the neighbouring farm and had the building consecrated. Since then, the tiny church has seen numerous christenings and burials, although a wedding might be pushing it. Inside is a single pew, seating four people, and standing room for six. Its annual service, needless to say, is held outside.

The actor JOHN THAW and his wife, actress SHEILA HANCOCK, bought a 17th-century house in Luckington, or Lucky, as it's known to the locals, in 1990. John loved it, and would hide away in it, curling up and shutting the world out. They lived there on a semi-permanent basis until Thaw's death in 2002. Sheila writes in her book *The Two of Us*:

'Today at the Post Office two photographers started snapping at us. John was feeling peaky and just sighed but I was like a wild animal. Luckington has never seen such an unseemly display!'

Good for her, I say.

A bit of Ancient History...

Avebury Ring is a henge – a stone circle enclosed by a bank and ditch – built over many centuries, beginning around 2600 BC. It actually consists of three circles, the outer circle being the largest of its kind in Europe and containing the two smaller stone circles within it, known as the Northern and Southern Circles. The stones came from the Marlborough Downs, and would have required remarkable effort to move. It's thought that there were originally hundreds of standing stones at Avebury, of which 30 remain today, set in shallow holes in the chalky ground. The heaviest, known as the Swindon Stone, weighs around 65 tonnes and after 4,500 years still balances on one corner, with only a small part anchored in the ground! A great obelisk once stood in the centre of the Southern Circle at 21 feet (6.5m) high, represented today by a concrete post.

Avebury was probably used in ceremonies concerning the cycle of life and death, and still holds religious importance for modern-day pagans and druids. It seems to have fallen out of use in the Iron Age and Roman periods, but a village grew up around the henge later in Saxon times, and eventually extended into it. Much of the modern-day village of Avebury is encircled by the monument, and the High Street still follows the Saxon 'herepath' or military road. Though several stones were toppled and buried by Christians in medieval times because they were pagan symbols, they were recovered in a 1930s project to reconstruct the site, which is open to the public today and attracts hordes of visitors, from both the UK and abroad.

Avebury Stones Creative Commons

The shape of the stones and circles could reveal something about their purpose. The fact that some of them are diamond-shaped and some form pillars has led to a theory that they symbolise male and female, and may have been related to fertility rites. The two small inner circles may have been for men and women to worship in separate spaces, may have served as public theatres for ceremonies, or may have represented the sun and moon.

Avebury forms part of the wider prehistoric landscape of Wiltshire, which includes such famous sites as **Stonehenge** and **Silbury Hill**

Silbury Hill Andy & Susan Caffrey

Stonehenge, one of the world's most iconic monuments, is another ring of ancient stones that stands on Salisbury Plain. It emerged over thousands of years, with the first part being built between 3000 and 2400 BC, when a ditch was dug with antler tools and chalk was built up to make a bank. Some 500 years later, sarsen stones from the Marlborough Downs were brought to make up the inner rings, along with the smaller bluestones, which came all the way from the Welsh Preseli Hills.

In 2000, volunteers came from as far away as Australia to take part in an attempt to move a three-tonne stone from Wales to Stonehenge, using only the tools and methods that we know would have been available in ancient times. However, when it came to crossing choppy waters near Milford Haven, the huge stone came loose from its straps and ended up at the bottom of the Bristol Channel! The failure of the mission reignited support for the idea that the stones might have been pushed to Wiltshire by glaciers.

Like other prehistoric monuments, Stonehenge is shrouded in myth and mystery. Some argue that it was an ancient Roman temple, while others suggest it was used to calculate the dates of eclipses. It may also have been used as a place of healing and ancestor worship. The stones are part of a landscape that's home to hundreds of burial mounds, and was almost certainly used for burials from very early times. However, the culture that created it left no records of its people or their methods, leaving us to wonder.

In the twentieth century, Stonehenge has been revived as a religious site, with New Age pagans and druids performing ceremonies there. For the most significant date in their calendar, the summer solstice, they are joined by thousands of visitors every year for a night of music and dancing around the stones, culminating in the sunrise over the Heel Stone on the morning of 21 June.

Silbury Hill in the Kennett valley, between Marlborough and Calne, is the tallest man-made mound in Europe and one of the largest on earth. At 130 feet (40m) high and covering over five acres, the prehistoric hill is of a similar size to the smaller of the Egyptian pyramids.

Crafted around 4,750 years ago from chalk and clay excavated from the local area, it would have taken an estimated 500 men working for 15 years to complete. Though its original purpose remains a mystery, it's been speculated that ancient rituals would have involved raising an elite group, perhaps a priesthood, above the heads of everyone else, to be seen for miles around, including at other monuments in the area. One legend says that the hill was made when the Devil, carrying a bag of soil with which to destroy the town of Marlborough, was stopped by priests from Avebury.

Stonehenge at the summer solstice Creative Commons

In the nineteenth century, residents of Overton and the surrounding villages held celebrations on top of the mound every Palm Sunday. In medieval times, the round top was flattened, suggesting a defensive purpose. Whatever its origins, this stunning monument has been many things to many people over the centuries.

White horses

Wiltshire is the county for white horses. There are or were at least 24 of these hill figures in Britain, with no fewer than 13 being in Wiltshire, and another white horse, the oldest of them all, is just over the border in Oxfordshire. Most of the white horses are chalk hill carvings, and the chalk downs of central Wiltshire make it an ideal place for these impressive landmarks.

Of the 13 known to have existed in Wiltshire, eight are still visible, while the others have either been lost completely, or are in a sense still there, under the turf, but have long since become overgrown and therefore no longer visible.

Contrary to popular belief, most white horses are not particularly ancient. Only the Uffington white horse in Oxfordshire is definitely prehistoric, being approximately 3,000 years old. Most of the others are believed to date from the last 300 years or so, though the hillside white horse can be a slippery creature, and the origins of some are impossible to establish with any certainty.

Literary Connections

Although he is mostly associated with neighbouring Dorset, the landscape of Wiltshire was also a key inspiration for the works of THOMAS HARDY (1840–1928). The county forms part of Hardy's 'Wessex', an imaginary English county in which all his major works are set. This land, which he called 'a merely realistic dream country', consisted of numerous real counties in south and south-west England, with Wiltshire corresponding to 'Mid-Wessex' in the novels. The town of Salisbury was renamed 'Melchester' for *Jude the Obscure* (1895).

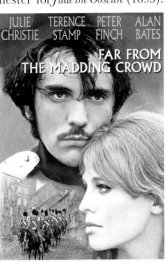

For the film version of his novel *Far From the Madding Crowd* (1967), the fictitious setting of Weatherbury was filmed in part in Devizes, with the Bear Hotel, Corn Exchange and St John's Church featuring in key scenes. In the final chapter of *Tess of the d'Urbervilles* (1892), the heroine stumbles upon Stonehenge in the dead of night and lies down to rest on the ancient stones.

Far from the Madding Crowd
www.freeclasicimages.com

In 1910, LADY ALDA HOARE of Stourhead, Wiltshire wrote to Hardy for an autographed copy of *Far From the Madding Crowd* (1874), and the regency library at Stourhead now houses a collection of letters and postcards documenting the 25 years of friendship that followed.

Another Victorian novelist, ANTHONY TROLLOPE (1815–82) set his *Barchester Chronicles* series in the fictional county of Barsetshire and the cathedral town of Barchester, based on Salisbury. He was sent by the Post Office in Ireland, where he worked, to England in 1851 to establish a postal network in the west of the country. Trollope spent 'two of the happiest years' of his life riding 40 miles a day on horseback to find routes for postmen to travel on foot. He writes in his autobiography of how, *'wandering in Salisbury one midsummer evening round the purlieus of the cathedral, I conceived the story of The Warden'*, the first novel in the Barsetshire series, which follows the lives and loves of the clergy and townspeople.

In his later years, *James Bond* author IAN FLEMING (1908–64) was a resident of the village of Sevenhampton outside Swindon. He and his family moved into the 16th-century manor Warneford Place in 1963, where Fleming planned to settle down and get involved in the local community, but unfortunately he died only a year later following a heart attack. He is buried in the parish church of St James.

Since Fleming's secret agent hero rose to fame, the Bond connection with Swindon has continued. In *A View to a Kill* (1984), the futuristic Renault building is the backdrop for scenes in which Bond (ROGER MOORE) and Sir Godfrey Tibbett (PATRICK MACNEE) try to stop the villain, played by CHRISTOPHER WALKEN, from destroying the world, and the Motorola factory was used in *The World Is Not Enough* (2000) as an oil pumping station. PIERCE BROSNAN even popped into the nearby **Plough Inn** for a pint of Arkell's during filming!

The Swindon area is now also home the only pub in the world called '*The Goldfinger*' ('The Goldie' to its regulars). It was opened in 1971 by Ian Fleming's widow, Ann, and seems a fitting tribute to the creator of a character who was as fond of a tipple as Bond is – although you're more likely to find real ale and pork scratchings here than martinis, shaken not stirred!

Author and Nobel Laureate WILLIAM GOLDING (1911–93) grew up in Marlborough, which he renamed 'Stilbourne' for the setting of his novel *The Pyramid* (1967). A teaching post at Bishop Wordsworth's School in Salisbury later in life coincided with his writing of *Lord of the Flies* (1954), where his adolescent male pupils presumably acted as inspiration for the reckless schoolboys of the disturbing tale. After living for some years in Salisbury, Golding moved to Bowerchalke in 1958, where he is now buried in the village churchyard.

A magazine published by CHARLES DICKENS in the 1850s, *Household Words*, popularised an epitaph that he attributed to the Wiltshire village of Pewsey. It still turns up in anthologies of epitaphs today – you can see why:

> Here lies the body of LADY O'LOONEY, Great Niece of Burke. Commonly called the sublime. She was bland, passionate and deeply religious, also she painted in water colours and sent several pictures to the Exhibition. She was first cousin of Lady Jones, and of such is the Kingdom of Heaven.

However, the rector of Pewsey at the time, THOMAS RAVENSHAW, was inspired to research the subject of epitaphs and in 1878 published his own collection, *Antiente Epitaphes*, a copy of which resides at the Wiltshire Archaeological Society at Devizes. In an appendix he laid to rest the ghost of Lady O'Looney, who had never been in Pewsey at all!

VIKRAM SETH (born 1952) is an Indian novelist, travel writer, poet, biographer and memoirist. He lives near Salisbury in the former home of poet George Herbert and can often be seen at literary and cultural events. His travel writing includes *From Heaven Lake: Travels Through Sinkiang and Tibet* and it won him the Thomas Cook Travel Book Award. Novels include *A Suitable Boy* (1993), which, at 1,349 pages and 591,552 words, is one of the longest novels ever published in a single volume in the English language!

Old Sarum is the site of the original city of Salisbury; it was founded in the Iron Age and occupied until the 16th century. Romans, Saxons and Normans have all left their mark. Part of the Domesday Book was written here, and on its completion it was to Sarum that KING WILLIAM I summoned all the landholders in England to swear their oath of allegiance. The international best seller *Sarum* by EDWARD RUTHERFURD is largely based in the Salisbury area and Old Sarum.

Pour me a pint, pull up a stool and I'll tell you a tale...

As you've probably started to notice, Wiltshire has very strong literary connections and, not surprisingly, these can often be linked to local pubs and inns. Here are a few examples. *(Personally, I suggest you visit them all to find out more for yourself!)*

Green Dragon, Alderbury. Early in *Martin Chuzzlewit*, DICKENS introduces a little Wiltshire village within easy journey of the fair old town of Salisbury. It lies a short distance off the main coaching road to London and has a snug alehouse, which he calls the *Blue Dragon*, where much of the action takes place. Nearby is a church with a tapering spire, a forge, a sparkling stream and a three-storey house where the architect *Mr Pecksniff* lives.

Two Wiltshire pubs claim to be the original for the Blue Dragon, this one and **The George** at Amesbury, but the George has little evidence to support its claim. The charming 15th-century **Green Dragon** is generally accepted as Dickens' model.

Waggon & Horses, Beckhampton. The A4 was once the main road linking Bristol and London, and the journey by horseback or stagecoach would take two days, crossing the coldest stretch – the Marlborough Downs at Beckhampton – at around the halfway point. On severe winter nights The Waggon and Horses was a most welcome sight and potential stop-over for weary travellers, including Charles Dickens. Dickens had a technique of inserting little stories into the narrative of his novels and in The Pickwick Papers he gives us a very amusing story of *Tom Smart the Bagman* and his strange encounter here with a haunted chair.

The Lamb at Hindon. This attractive old stone building with its tiled roof sits in the middle of the charming village of Hindon and dates back to the 12th century.

The Lamb at Hindon Creative Commons

It's known to have been an inn in the 16th century and by 1870 was already well established as a coaching house, supplying 300 post horses for the London and West Country route.

W.H. HUDSON, novelist and masterly writer on the natural world, stayed here for several weeks in the spring and summer of 1909 when researching his most famous book *A Shepherd's Life* (see p75). Over a century has passed since Hudson wrote those notes but the Lamb has changed little. It's a different story for the village. The road below Hudson's window was then the main A30 artery from Salisbury to Exeter. Today's travellers to and from the West Country speed along the A303 a mile or so to the north of this now tranquil spot.

George Inn, Mere. On 6 October 1651 a party of riders, including a tall, dark stranger, stopped at the George Inn for refreshment. The disguised stranger was CHARLES STUART, the future King of England, on the run after his army's defeat at the Battle of Worcester. The Victorian novelist HARRISON AINSWORTH dramatised this event in his novel *Boscobel*, or *the Royal Oak* which tells the story of Charles flight. The whole of Chapter 22 is set in the inn and is entitled '*How they dined at the George at Mere, and how the host related his dream*'.

The Inn was built in 1580 and renamed **The Talbot** through the 19th century until recently, from the crest of the Grove family who owned it. In a dining room adjacent to the main bar is a portrait of Charles II together with a framed text detailing the King's visit. It seems likely that Ainsworth visited Mere while researching the book as he includes these observations:

> '*While riding out of Mere, they gazed at the fine old church with its lofty tower, at the ancient market-house, and at the lofty mound on which were some vestiges of a castle, built in the reign of Henry III.*'

Cathedral Hotel, Salisbury. In 1909 DOROTHY LEIGH SAYERS was sent as a boarder to The Godolphin School in Salisbury, where she won a scholarship to Somerville College, Oxford. She eventually became a London-based advertising copywriter and in the early 1920s started work on her first novel, *Whose Body?* which introduced LORD PETER WIMSEY. With his signature monocle and somewhat foppish air, Wimsey appeared in 11 novels and several short stories. In *Whose Body?* we find Wimsey having lunch in the Minster Hotel, Salisbury, and quizzing the waiter about a local solicitor whom he suspects of murder. This scene actually takes place at the Cathedral Hotel, which in 1924 would not have been the first choice for a Lord to dine – given the fact that the splendid Red Lion stands immediately opposite. Sayers tells us that it was the proximity to Milford Hill (the suspect's place of business) that induced Lord Peter to lunch at the Minster Hotel rather than the White Hart or some other more picturesquely situated hostel. The truth is that, although Dorothy Sayers thought her readers wanted to know about the aristocracy, it was not a world she was familiar with. Many of her characters are scholarly but financially pinched middle-class professionals like her, who would have been more comfortable dining at the Cathedral Hotel.

Red Lion, Salisbury. In Thomas Hardy's story *The Hand of Ethelberta* the characters disperse to two 'Melchester' hotels, which still exist today in Salisbury. The old and jealous Lord Mountclere, anxious to test the fidelity of his fiancée – the young and captivating Ethelberta Petherwin – follows her into the town: 'as far as the Red Lion Hotel, she turned towards it with her companion, and being shown to a room, the two sisters shut themselves in. Lord Mountclere paused and entered the White Hart, the rival hotel to the Red Lion, which stood in an adjoining street.'

It was here also here that Phillotson in *Jude the Obscure* stayed before his marriage. The Red Lion, famous for its creeper-clad courtyard, was built over 750 years ago to house the draughtsmen working on the design of nearby Salisbury Cathedral. It's believed to be the oldest purpose-built hotel in Britain, and evidence to support this came to light recently when a medieval fireplace was exposed during the refurbishment of one of the bedrooms in the original wing of the hotel. It is believed to date from around 1220, when work started on the Cathedral.

By the 1700s the Red Lion had become a flourishing coaching Inn and was a main terminus for regular mail coach services, linking London and the West Country. There are fine examples of wattle and daub and painted plaster walls dating from the 13th and 14th centuries and an impressive collection of antiques, including a china violin and the unique Skeleton Organ Clock.

The Red Lion Creative Commons

White Hart, Salisbury. The White Hart which dominates St John Street was built on the site of an earlier inn dating from the time of Henry VII. While lodging nearby, faking the symptoms of leprosy and publicly refusing food, SIR WALTER RALEIGH secretly obtained a leg of mutton and some loaves from the White Hart. The deception was a ploy to buy him some time while he worked on his '*Apology for the Voyage to Guiana*', which Raleigh hoped would placate KING JAMES I following the failure of the expedition.

Much of CHARLES DICKENS' *Martin Chuzzlewit* is set in and around Salisbury. It was in the White Hart that Martin and Tom Pinch were entertained to a sumptuous dinner by John Westlock, who ordered everything they had ever dreamed of. Dickens begins his wonderful description of the hostelry and the meal with these words: *'A Famous Inn! The hall a very grove of dead game and dangling joints of mutton'.*

Vamous volk of Wiltshire

The architect CHRISTOPHER WREN (1632–1723) was born in the village of East Knowle, where his father was the rector. Christopher was born in lodgings above a shop, where the family had been forced to move temporarily after a fire at the Rectory. Wren is most famous for designing buildings in London after the Great Fire of 1666 (including the beautiful St Paul's Cathedral) but he also recommended to his friend Bishop Seth Ward that the spire of Salisbury Cathedral be strengthened. The design of Farley Church in Wiltshire may have been influenced by Wren because he knew both the builder and the sponsor.

MICHAEL CRAWFORD was born Michael Patrick Dumbell-Smith in Salisbury in 1942. The comedy actor is famous for playing Frank Spencer in the television series *Some Mothers*

Do 'Ave 'Em. He's also a singer and has starred in musicals such as *Billy* and won an Olivier Award for his performance of the Phantom in ANDREW LLOYD WEBBER's *Phantom of the Opera*. He received an OBE in 1988.

In the churchyard at **Alvediston** is the grave of ANTHONY EDEN, first Earl of Avon (1897–1977), the British Prime Minister brought down by the Suez crisis of 1956.

South of Marlborough is **Martinsell Hill**, the favourite viewpoint of the Old Marlburian art historian and Stalinist spy ANTHONY BLUNT (1907–83). His ashes were scattered on the hillside there.

Marlborough vies with Stockton-on-Tees and Appleby for the widest high street in England. The famous college stands on the site of an old castle and it's said that Merlin the Wizard is buried in the school grounds under Maerl's Barrow.

Born JOHN TIMOTHY ROTHWELL in 1954, the eco campaigner and neo-druid changed his name by deed poll to Arthur Uther Pendragon. He was crowned the Raised Druid King of England in 1998. He is known for his battles with English Heritage to allow legal entry to Stonehenge for the summer and winter solstice. He won and in 2000, full public access was granted for these events. Arthur also stood for election in Salisbury in 2010 as an independent candidate.

Actor JOSEPH FIENNES (born 1970) is the youngest of six siblings. He was born in Salisbury and went to Swan School for Boys (now Leehurst Swan School). At 11, he continued his studies at Bishop Wordsworth's School. Film roles include William Shakespeare in *Shakespeare in Love* and Martin Luther in *Luther*.

Born in Swindon in 1982, BILLIE PIPER started her career as a pop singer, later turning to acting. She was the youngest ever artist to debut at number one in the UK singles chart, which she achieved with *'Because We Want To'*. Her most famous acting role is as Rose Tyler in *Doctor Who*. She was married for six years to DJ Chris Evans, and later married the actor Laurence Fox.

Hungry for More...?

WELL, DEAR READER, we've reached the end of our short journey together. I hope you've enjoyed reading this little book as much as I've enjoyed writing it!

Anyone who'd like to delve deeper into the world of Wiltshire dialect could do worse than obtain themselves a copy of *Marnin' Moonrakers! – A Celebration of Wiltshire Dialect*, by KEITH BURGE and TOM MILLS. It's a very accessible, light-hearted and often extremely funny read, described as *'a treasure trove of local folk history, a survival guide to the linguistic jungle of the Wiltshire dialect … capturing the warmth and humour of those who live there now'*.

For those of you interested in finding out more about rural life in Wiltshire during the 19th century, I can thoroughly recommend W.H. HUDSON's *A Shepherd's Life: Impressions of the South Wiltshire Downs*. This utterly engaging (I read it in one sitting!) history of rural life in Wiltshire focuses on head shepherd, CALEB BAWCOMBE. The author re-tells many stories that the old shepherd remembers from the mid-19th century. Both the stories and the language used to tell them paint a picture of a rural idyll that sadly has since been lost; luckily for us, though, the author (who wrote his book in 1910) took the time to sit with Bawcombe and document this important rural history. The natural history, the study of farming and the observations of characters – both human and animal – make this book a real treasure.

And finally, *Small Talk in Wiltshire*, collected and presented by JOHN CHANDLER, is a fascinating and entertaining exploration of *'all manner of obscure printed and documentary material relating to Wiltshire literature'.*

HAPPY READING!

Bibliography

A Shepherd's Life: Impressions of the South Wiltshire Downs, W.H. HUDSON 1910, CreateSpace Independent Publishing Platform, 2013

Glossary of Words Used In The County Of Wiltshire, GEORGE EDWARD DARTNELL and THE REV. EDWARD HUNGERFORD GODDARD, Published For The English Dialect Society By Henry Frowde, Oxford University Press Warehouse, 1893.

I Never Knew That About England, CHRISTOPHER WINN, Random House Group, 2008.

Marnin' Moonrakers! KEITH BURGE and TOM MILLS, Countryside Books, 2008.

Small Talk in Wiltshire, JOHN CHANDLER, Ex Libris Press, 1992.

The Two of Us: My Life with John Thaw, SHEILA HANCOCK, Bloomsbury Publishing, 2005.

Websites accessed December 2014 and January 2015

archive.org/stream/glossaryofwordsu18dartuoft/
glossaryofwordsu18dartuoft_djvu.txt
en.wikipedia.org/wiki/Anthony_Trollope
en.wikipedia.org/wiki/M%C3%A1el_Dub
en.wikipedia.org/wiki/Salisbury
en.wikipedia.org/wiki/Silbury_Hill http://www.stonehenge.
co.uk/avebury.php

www.avebury-web.co.uk/silbury_hill.html

www.bbc.co.uk/wiltshire/content/articles/2005/01/13/
voices_dialect_moonrakers_130105_feature.shtml

www.bbc.co.uk/wiltshire/content/articles/2005/01/13/
voices_placenames_130105_feature.shtml

www.bbc.co.uk/wiltshire/entertainment/days_out/thomas_
hardy_stourhead.shtml

www.brlsi.org/node/18153

www.cotswoldsadventures.co.uk/lacock-village/

www.dailymail.co.uk/news/article-2320150/Britains-
smallest-church-measuring-13ft-11ft-holds-annual-service-
outdoors-theres-room-flock-inside.html

www.domesdaybook.co.uk/places.html

www.english-heritage.org.uk/daysout/properties/avebury/
history-and-research/

www.english-heritage.org.uk/daysout/properties/
stonehenge/discover/

www.english-heritage.org.uk/daysout/travel-trade/themes-
ideas/literary-connections/

www.gazetteandherald.co.uk/news/5070463.Flying_start_
to_Malmesbury_s_celebrations_for_Eilmer/

www.historic-uk.com/CultureUK/The-Moonrakers/

www.homesteadbb.free-online.co.uk/wilts.html

www.horologica.co.uk/horology/Salisbury.html http://
en.wikipedia.org/wiki/Salisbury_cathedral_clock

www.metmuseum.org/toah/works-of-art/1997.382.1

www.movie-locations.com/movies/f/Far_From_The_
Madding_Crowd.html

www.salisburycathedral.org.uk/magna-carta-how-did-
magna-carta-come-about/salisbury-connection

www.salisburycathedral.org.uk/visit-literary-and-film-
links/barchester-chronicles-0

www.swindonweb.
com/?m=2&s=87&ss=91&c=2038&t=Swindon%20
written%20in%20James%20Bond%20history

www.swindonweb.com/woottonbassett/history.htm

www.telegraph.co.uk/news/earth/7955868/Crop-circle-
conundrum.html www.manchester.com/features/crop.php

www.theguardian.com/artanddesign/2003/feb/07/art.
artsfeatures

www.trollopesociety.org/barset.php

www.visitoruk.com/Marlborough/aldbourne-C592-V14420.
html

www.visitwiltshire.co.uk/ideas-and-inspiration/crop-circles

www.wessexarch.co.uk/files/Learning/avebury_teachers_
kit/information_sheet_for_avebury_henge_and_west_
kennet_avenue.pdf www.bbc.co.uk/wiltshire/moonraking/
landscape_stonehenge.shtml

www.wiltshiremuseum.org.uk/news/index.
php?Action=8&id=134&page=0

Available now

Black Country Dialect

Bristol Dialect

Cockney Dialect

Cornish Dialect

Derbyshire Dialect

Devon Dialect

Essex Dialect

Glaswegian Dialect

Hampshire Dialect

Kentish Dialect

Lancashire Dialect

Liverpool Dialect

Manchester Dialect

Newcastle Dialect

Norfolk Dialect

Somerset Dialect

Suffolk Dialect

Sussex Dialect

Warwickshire Dialect

Yorkshire Dialect

Available in 2015

Evolving English WordBank

Lincolnshire Dialect

Dorset Dialect

Scottish Dialects

The Cotswolds Dialect

The Lake District Dialect

Nottinghamshire Dialect

Leicestershire Dialect

See website for more details: bradwellbooks.com